Table of Contents

Navigating Your Future: A Beginner's Guide to Social Security

Property of

Elysian Pinnacle

A Personal Journey Through the Tapestry of Social Security

Before I start, let me share a story that encapsulates the essence of Social Security and its impact on individuals.

In my years as a Social Security advisor, I've had the privilege of witnessing the transformative power of this program in the lives of countless individuals. One story that stands out is that of Mr. and Mrs. Anderson, a couple who approached me with a mix of anticipation and uncertainty.

Mr. Anderson, a dedicated factory worker, had spent decades contributing to Social Security. The Andersons were approaching retirement, a phase that should have been a celebration of their hard work and dedication. However, a cloud of uncertainty hung over them as they navigated the complexities of retirement planning.

As we sat down to discuss their options, I could see the relief on their faces as we demystified the intricacies of Social Security. Understanding the nuances of retirement benefits, spousal benefits, and the importance of timing brought clarity to their financial landscape. Social Security wasn't just a bureaucratic concept; it was a tailored plan designed to suit their unique needs.

A few years later, life threw an unexpected curveball. Mr. Anderson faced a health challenge that led to his inability to work. In these trying times, the Disability Benefits component of Social Security became their financial lifeline. The support provided not only alleviated the financial strain but also allowed the Andersons to focus on what truly mattered – Mr. Anderson's recovery and their continued well-being.

Tragically, Mr. Anderson passed away, leaving Mrs. Anderson in the wake of grief and financial uncertainty. However, the Survivor Benefits offered by Social Security ensured that she was not left alone to navigate this challenging chapter. The steady stream of financial support allowed her the time and space needed to adjust to a new reality without the added stress of financial instability.

The Andersons' story is not unique, but it exemplifies the multifaceted role that Social Security plays in people's lives. It's a story of resilience, support, and the profound impact that a well-structured social insurance program can have on individuals and families.

As a Social Security advisor, I find immense satisfaction in being part of these journeys. It's not just about numbers and regulations; it's about empowering individuals to navigate life's uncertainties with the assurance that comes from a solid financial plan. The Andersons' story is a testament to the enduring promise of Social Security – a promise that extends beyond retirement, reaching into the realms of disability and providing solace in times of loss.

In every consultation, I am reminded that Social Security is not just a program; it's a lifeline, a safety net that weaves itself into the very fabric of people's lives, providing a sense of security and peace of mind. It's a privilege to guide individuals like the Andersons through the intricacies of Social Security, ensuring that their journey is not just financially secure but also imbued with the dignity and support they deserve.

INTRODUCTION: UNLOCKING THE DOORS TO YOUR FINANCIAL SECURITY

"Since the day you took your first step into the workforce, a silent companion has been by your side, working tirelessly to secure your financial future. Have you ever wondered about that steady force ensuring a safety net beneath you, ready to catch you when the time comes to hang up your hat and retire? Enter the world of Social Security, a crucial aspect of your financial journey that often sits quietly in the background until its importance takes center stage.

Imagine a future where your hard work transforms into a reliable source of income, supporting you through the golden years of retirement. Picture a safety net that shields you and your loved ones in times of disability or unforeseen loss. This isn't a distant dream but a reality crafted by Social Security, a program designed to bring financial security and peace of mind to individuals across the nation.

Unraveling the Mystery

What is Social Security, and how does it shape your financial landscape? Social Security is more than just a government program; it's a promise, a pact between you and the future. It's the embodiment of societal support, ensuring that as you contribute to the workforce, a fund is set aside to provide financial assistance when you need it most.

A Journey Through Time

Let's take a step back and explore the roots of Social Security. Envision a time when the world faced economic uncertainties, and the idea of financial security for the elderly, disabled, and survivors gained prominence. In 1935, amidst the challenges of the Great Depression, the Social Security Act was born, a beacon of hope that would forever alter the financial landscape for millions.

Your Personal Financial Guardian

You might be wondering, who is eligible for these benefits? How does one tap into this reservoir of financial support? The eligibility criteria vary, covering retirees, individuals with disabilities, and surviving family members. Your journey with Social Security begins when you decide to embark on the path of retirement or face unexpected challenges.

The Three Pillars

Picture Social Security as a three-pillar structure, each pillar supporting a different phase of your life. The first pillar is Retirement Benefits, symbolizing the end of your working years and the beginning of a well-deserved rest. The second pillar, Disability Benefits, steps in when life takes an unexpected turn, providing a financial lifeline during periods of incapacity. Lastly, the third pillar, Survivor Benefits, ensures that even in the face of loss, financial security remains for those left behind.

The Adventure Begins

Are you ready to embark on this adventure of understanding and harnessing the power of Social Security? In the chapters that follow, we'll delve into the nitty-gritty details, from eligibility criteria to the calculation of benefits, demystifying the complexities and empowering you to make informed decisions.

Your journey through Social Security is more than just a financial expedition; it's a voyage towards securing a future filled with peace, prosperity, and the freedom to savor the fruits of your labor. So, let's dive into the world of Social Security, unravel its secrets, and pave the way for a financially secure tomorrow."

1.1 What is Social Security?

Social Security is not just a bureaucratic term or a complex system of rules; it's a lifeline, a safety net woven by the collective commitment of society. At its core, Social Security is a government program designed to provide financial support to individuals in various stages of life, ensuring a level of economic security when they need it most. It operates as a social insurance program, pooling contributions from workers and employers to create a fund that offers benefits to retirees, disabled individuals, and surviving family members.

In simpler terms, Social Security is your financial companion, ready to offer a helping hand when life takes unexpected turns or when the time comes to bid farewell to the workforce. It's a promise made by society to safeguard its members, promoting the well-being of individuals and their families.

1.2 Purpose and Importance

The purpose of Social Security extends far beyond a mere retirement plan. It serves as a cornerstone of social welfare, addressing the financial challenges that individuals may encounter due to aging, disability, or the loss of a breadwinner. The importance of Social Security lies in its ability to foster economic stability, reduce poverty among vulnerable populations, and promote a sense of security and dignity in retirement.

By providing a reliable income stream, Social Security allows retirees to maintain a decent standard of living and contribute to the overall well-being of communities. Moreover, it offers protection to individuals with disabilities, ensuring they have the financial support needed to navigate life's challenges. The survivor benefits component adds another layer of security, offering financial assistance to family members left behind in the event of a worker's death.

In essence, Social Security is a testament to the collective responsibility we share as a society. It reflects the values of compassion, solidarity, and the belief that everyone deserves a measure of financial security throughout their life journey.

1.3 Historical Overview

To truly appreciate the significance of Social Security, we must journey back to the turbulent times of the Great Depression. In 1935, in response to the economic hardships faced by the nation, President Franklin D. Roosevelt signed the Social Security Act into law. This landmark legislation marked the birth of Social Security and established a comprehensive system of benefits aimed at addressing the economic insecurities prevalent during that era.

The original Social Security Act encompassed retirement benefits for workers, unemployment insurance, aid to dependent children, and a range of public health initiatives. Over the years, the program evolved, expanding its scope and refining its mechanisms to adapt to the changing needs of society.

Today, Social Security stands as a testament to the enduring commitment of a nation to provide for its citizens. It has weathered economic shifts, legislative changes, and societal transformations, remaining a bedrock of financial stability for millions of Americans. Understanding this historical context is vital as we navigate the intricacies of Social Security, recognizing its roots in a collective desire to build a more secure and equitable future for all.

2. Eligibility and Enrollment: Navigating Your Path to Security

In the journey toward Social Security benefits, the first crucial step is understanding who is eligible to embark on this path. It's not just a matter of age; it's about recognizing the diverse situations that life may throw your way.

2.1 Who is Eligible for Social Security Benefits?

Have you contributed to the workforce? If so, you've likely been weaving the threads of your Social Security safety net. Social Security eligibility isn't restricted to a select few; it's a promise that extends to most workers, their spouses, and even dependent children.

Key Eligibility Categories:

- **Retirees:** Individuals who have worked and contributed to Social Security for a specified period.
- **Disabled Individuals:** Those facing a qualifying disability that hinders substantial work.

- **Survivors:** Family members eligible for benefits in the unfortunate event of a worker's death.

Understanding your eligibility is like unlocking a door to financial security. It's a recognition of your commitment to the workforce and society's reciprocal commitment to your well-being.

2.2 Age Requirements for Retirement Benefits

Picture this: the sun setting on your career, and a new chapter of life awaits. But when is the ideal moment to turn that page? Age matters when it comes to retirement benefits.

Key Age Milestones:

- **Full Retirement Age (FRA):** This is the age when you can receive full Social Security retirement benefits. It varies based on your birth year.
- **Early Retirement:** You can choose to start receiving reduced benefits as early as age 62.
- **Delayed Retirement:** By delaying benefits beyond FRA, you can enhance your monthly payments.

As your Social Security advisor, I often ask clients: What's your ideal retirement age? How can we tailor your benefits to align with your life goals?

Making Enrollment Painless

Once you grasp your eligibility and ideal retirement age, the next step is enrollment. Thankfully, the process has become remarkably user-friendly.

Options for Enrollment:

1. Online Application: A convenient and efficient way to apply from the comfort of your home.

2. In-Person Application: Visit your local Social Security office for personalized assistance.

3. Phone Application: Speak directly to a Social Security representative.

Enrolling in Social Security is not just a bureaucratic step; it's a moment of empowerment. It's the initiation of a journey toward financial security tailored to your unique circumstances.

Remember, eligibility and enrollment are more than technicalities; they're the first steps toward a future where you can savor the fruits of your labor. As your guide in this journey, my role is to simplify, clarify, and ensure you embark on this path with confidence and understanding.

2.3 Disability Eligibility Criteria: Paving the Way for Support

Life is unpredictable, and sometimes unexpected challenges may alter our course. Social Security stands as a steadfast companion, offering a safety net for those facing disabilities. Let's delve into the criteria that open the doors to Disability Benefits.

Understanding Disability Eligibility

Have you ever wondered what happens if life takes an unexpected turn, and you find yourself unable to work due to a disability? Social Security is here for you, providing a financial lifeline.

Key Criteria for Disability Benefits:

1. Qualifying Medical Condition: A condition that prevents substantial work and is expected to last at least a year or result in death.

2. Work Credits: The accumulation of work credits based on your employment history, demonstrating your contribution to Social Security.

Navigating the world of disability benefits can be complex, but it's also a testament to society's commitment to supporting individuals in their moments of need.

2.4 Survivor Benefits Eligibility: A Beacon in Times of Loss

In the face of loss, financial stability becomes a crucial pillar. Survivor Benefits are designed to provide support to the loved ones left behind. Who is eligible for this vital lifeline?

Key Eligibility Factors:

1. Relationship to the Deceased: Spouses, children, and in some cases, dependent parents may be eligible.
2. Deceased's Work History: The deceased individual must have worked long enough and paid Social Security taxes for family members to qualify.

Survivor Benefits ensure that even in the darkest moments, a financial cushion exists to ease the burden.

2.5 How to Enroll in Social Security: Your Personal Roadmap

Now that we've explored the eligibility criteria, let's chart the course for enrollment. This isn't just paperwork; it's your gateway to a future where financial security is more than a promise—it's a reality.

Seamless Enrollment Process

1. Online Application: Embrace the convenience of the digital era by applying online through the official Social Security website. It's a user-friendly platform designed to make your journey smoother.

2. In-Person Assistance: Sometimes, a personal touch is invaluable. Visit your local Social Security office, where knowledgeable staff can guide you through the application process and address any questions.

3. Phone Application: If you prefer the human touch but can't visit in person, a phone application allows you to connect with a Social Security representative who will assist you in completing the necessary steps.

Enrollment is not just a formality; it's your initiation into a system built to safeguard your future. As your Social Security advisor, my role is to ensure this process is as straightforward as possible, empowering you to step confidently into a future of financial security.

3. Types of Social Security Benefits: A Palette of Security

Social Security unfolds like a canvas, painting a picture of financial security across various stages of life. Let's explore the two primary strokes on this canvas – Retirement Benefits and Disability Benefits.

3.1 Retirement Benefits: Harvesting the Fruits of Your Labor

Picture this: the moment you bid farewell to the workforce, a new chapter begins. Retirement Benefits are not just a financial reward; they're the culmination of your dedication and hard work.

Key Elements of Retirement Benefits:

1. Full Retirement Age (FRA): The age at which you can receive full benefits, varying based on your birth year.
2. Early Retirement: The option to start receiving reduced benefits as early as age 62.
3. Delayed Retirement: By waiting beyond FRA, you can increase your monthly benefits.

Retirement Benefits are more than just numbers on a check; they're the foundation of a life where you dictate the rhythm.

3.2 Disability Benefits: A Safety Net in Unexpected Storms

Life is unpredictable, and sometimes, storms may alter our course. Disability Benefits are not just financial support; they're a lifeline for those facing unforeseen challenges.

Crucial Aspects of Disability Benefits:

1. Qualifying Conditions: A medical condition preventing substantial work, expected to last at least a year or result in death.
2. Work Credits: The accumulation of credits based on your employment history, ensuring you've contributed to the system.

Disability Benefits provide financial stability during moments when you need it most, embodying the essence of societal support.

The Interplay of Retirement and Disability

Have you ever considered the interconnected nature of these benefits? Retirement and Disability Benefits often dance together on life's stage, supporting individuals through different acts of their journey.

Transitioning Between Benefits:

- From Disability to Retirement: As you approach full retirement age, your Disability Benefits seamlessly transition into Retirement Benefits.
- Early Retirement Due to Disability: In some cases, individuals may opt for early retirement due to disability, navigating a unique pathway through the Social Security landscape.

Understanding this interplay ensures a smooth transition between chapters of your life, each supported by the intricate tapestry of Social Security benefits.

As your advisor, I often guide individuals in aligning these benefits with their life goals, ensuring that the symphony of Retirement and Disability Benefits creates a harmonious and secure melody for their future.

3.3 Survivor Benefits: A Closer Look

Have you ever pondered what happens when a family faces the profound loss of a breadwinner? Survivor Benefits step in, transforming a moment of grief into a time of financial security.

Eligibility for Survivor Benefits:

1. Relationship to the Deceased: Spouses, children, and in some cases, dependent parents may qualify.

2. Deceased's Work History: The deceased individual must have worked long enough and paid Social Security taxes for family members to be eligible.

Crucial Aspects of Survivor Benefits:

- Full Survivor Benefits: Available at full retirement age, providing maximum financial support.

- Early Survivor Benefits: Available as early as age 60, though at a reduced rate.

Understanding Survivor Benefits isn't just about paperwork; it's about ensuring that those left behind have a financial cushion during a challenging transition.

3.4 Spousal Benefits: Sharing the Social Security Tapestry

Picture a retirement where both partners can bask in the benefits of their combined work history. Spousal Benefits are more than individual; they're a shared journey towards financial security.

Key Elements of Spousal Benefits:

1. Marriage Duration: Typically, a spouse is eligible for benefits based on the other's work record if the marriage has lasted at least one year.

2. Full Spousal Benefits: Up to 50% of the higher-earning spouse's benefit, available at full retirement age.

3. Early Spousal Benefits: Available as early as age 62, though at a reduced rate.

Navigating Spousal Benefits involves understanding the dynamics of a partnership and optimizing benefits to create a unified financial plan for both individuals.

3.5 Dependent Benefits: Nurturing the Future

Children are the heartbeats of the future, and Social Security extends its embrace to support them through

Dependent Benefits. It's more than financial aid; it's an investment in the next generation.

Crucial Aspects of Dependent Benefits:

1. Eligible Dependents: Children, adopted children, and in some cases, stepchildren may qualify.

2. Age Limitations: Benefits typically extend until a dependent child turns 18 (or 19 if still in high school).

3. Disabled Adult Children: In certain situations, disabled adult children may continue to receive benefits.

Understanding the intricacies of Dependent Benefits ensures that the financial well-being of your loved ones is secured, creating a legacy of support.

As your Social Security advisor, I weave these benefits into a comprehensive plan, recognizing that each element plays a unique role in the tapestry of your financial security. Together, we navigate the complexities, ensuring that the symphony of Survivor, Spousal, and Dependent Benefits harmonizes into a melody of stability for you and your loved ones.

4. Calculating Social Security Benefits: Unraveling the Financial Puzzle

Calculating Social Security benefits involves understanding the intricate puzzle pieces that determine your financial future. Let's delve into the foundational elements – your Earnings Record, Work Credits, and the pivotal Full Retirement Age (FRA).

4.1 Earnings Record and Work Credits: Your Financial Building Blocks

Think of your Earnings Record and Work Credits as the foundation of your financial house. These elements not only reflect your dedication to the workforce but also play a crucial role in shaping your Social Security benefits.

Understanding Earnings Record:

- **Every Dollar Counts:** Social Security benefits are based on your lifetime earnings. Your Earnings Record is a comprehensive history of your income over the years.

- Indexing for Inflation: Earnings are adjusted to account for changes in wage levels, ensuring a fair reflection of your lifetime contributions.

Crucial Role of Work Credits:

- **Earning Work Credits:** You earn credits based on your work history and income. In 2022, one credit is earned for every $1,470 of earnings, with a maximum of four credits per year.

- **Qualifying for Benefits:** The number of credits you need depends on your age at the time of disability, retirement, or survivorship.

Understanding the nuances of your Earnings Record and Work Credits lays the groundwork for accurate benefit calculations.

4.2 Full Retirement Age (FRA): The Pinnacle of Benefits

The concept of Full Retirement Age (FRA) is like reaching the summit of a mountain – it marks the optimal point for reaping the rewards of your Social Security benefits.

Defining Full Retirement Age:

- Varied Ages: FRA isn't a one-size-fits-all concept; it varies based on your birth year. For those born between 1943 and 1954, FRA is 66.

- Gradual Increase: For individuals born after 1954, FRA gradually increases, reaching 67 for those born in 1960 and later.

Significance of Full Retirement Age:

- Maximum Benefits: Waiting until FRA ensures that you receive your full Social Security retirement benefits.
- Early or Delayed Options: You can choose to retire as early as age 62 (with reduced benefits) or delay retirement until after FRA (with increased benefits).

Understanding the dynamics of Full Retirement Age empowers you to make informed decisions about the timing of your retirement, ensuring maximum financial security.

4.3 Primary Insurance Amount (PIA): Decoding the Heart of Your Benefits

Behind the curtain of Social Security benefits, the Primary Insurance Amount (PIA) stands as a central figure, determining the core of your financial support. Let's unravel the mysteries of PIA and explore how it shapes your benefits.

PIA is not just an acronym; it's the heartbeat of your Social Security benefits. Understanding its essence is like holding the key to unlocking the full potential of your financial security.

Defining Primary Insurance Amount:

- **Essence of PIA:** PIA is the baseline amount of your Social Security benefit, representing what you'd receive if you claim benefits at your Full Retirement Age (FRA).
- **Calculation Basis:** It's calculated based on your highest-earning years, adjusted for inflation.

Factors Influencing PIA:

- **Earnings Record:** The higher your lifetime earnings, the higher your PIA.
- **Full Retirement Age (FRA):** PIA is maximized when you claim benefits at FRA.
- **Benefit Formula:** A complex formula involving specific percentages of portions of your average indexed monthly earnings (AIME).

Understanding PIA is pivotal, as it sets the stage for the adjustments that follow in your Social Security benefits journey.

4.4 Adjustments for Early or Delayed Retirement: The Timing Effect

Timing is everything in the realm of Social Security benefits. Adjustments for Early or Delayed Retirement add a dynamic element to the equation, allowing you to tailor your benefits to fit your unique life circumstances.

Early Retirement Adjustments:

- **Claiming Benefits at 62:** If you opt for early retirement, your benefits are reduced. For those with an FRA of 66, the reduction is approximately 25%.

Delayed Retirement Credits:

- **Beyond Full Retirement Age:** Delaying your retirement past FRA results in increased benefits. For every year you delay, you receive an additional 8% in benefits, up to age 70.

Understanding these adjustments empowers you to make strategic decisions, aligning your retirement timing with your financial goals.

4.5 Maximizing Your Benefits: Crafting Your Financial Legacy

Maximizing your Social Security benefits is not just a financial strategy; it's an art. It involves carefully orchestrating the elements we've explored to create a harmonious melody of financial security.

Strategies for Maximization:

1. Claiming at FRA: Opting for benefits at FRA ensures you receive your full PIA, striking a balance between early and delayed options.

2. Delayed Retirement: For those able to wait, delaying retirement until age 70 results in maximum benefits, providing a robust foundation for your later years.

3. Spousal Coordination: Coordinating benefits with your spouse can enhance the overall financial picture, allowing you both to maximize your Social Security potential.

Maximizing your benefits is not a one-size-fits-all endeavor; it's a personalized strategy crafted to align with your unique financial journey.

5. Applying for Social Security Benefits: A Seamless Digital Journey

Embarking on the path to Social Security benefits is now more accessible than ever, thanks to the convenience of the online application process. Let's explore the digital landscape, where your journey to financial security begins with just a few clicks.

5.1 Online Application Process: Navigating the Virtual Gateway

In a world where convenience is king, the online application process for Social Security benefits stands as a testament to the digital age. Imagine applying for your benefits from the comfort of your home, and let's walk through the steps of this user-friendly virtual gateway.

1. Visit the Official Social Security Website:
- Open your preferred web browser and navigate to the official Social Security Administration (SSA) website: [Social Security Online](https://www.ssa.gov/).

2. Create a Social Security Account:

- If you haven't already, create a personal account on the SSA website. This account will be your secure portal for managing your benefits.

3. Verify Your Identity:

- To ensure the security of your information, the online application process requires identity verification. Be prepared to provide personal details and answer security questions.

4. Complete the Application:

- Once your identity is verified, proceed to the online application. The digital form will guide you through the necessary fields, collecting essential information about your work history, personal details, and benefit preferences.

5. Review and Submit:

- Take a moment to review the information you've entered. Ensure accuracy, as this will play a crucial role in determining your benefits. Once satisfied, submit your application electronically.

6. Receive Confirmation:

- After submitting your application, you'll receive a confirmation message. Keep this confirmation for your records.

7. Follow Up on Your Application:
- Use your online account to track the status of your application. The SSA website provides regular updates on the progress of your benefits processing.

The online application process is not just a matter of filling out forms; it's your passport to a future of financial security. As your advisor, I encourage you to embrace the simplicity and convenience of this digital journey, ensuring that your application is a seamless step toward unlocking the benefits you've earned.

5.2 In-Person Application: A Guided Approach to Security

While the online application process provides a convenient avenue for many, the option for an in-person application offers a personalized touch for those who prefer a more hands-on approach. Let's explore the steps involved in applying for Social Security benefits in person.

Choosing to apply for Social Security benefits in person brings a human touch to the process. Whether seeking guidance or preferring direct assistance, the in-person application option provides a guided approach.

1. Locate Your Nearest Social Security Office:

- Use the Social Security Administration's website to find the office nearest to you. [Find Your Local Office](https://secure.ssa.gov/ICON/main.jsp)

2. Schedule an Appointment:

- While some offices accept walk-ins, scheduling an appointment ensures dedicated time for your application. You can do this through the SSA website or by calling the local office.

3. Gather Required Documents:

- Before your appointment, ensure you have all necessary documentation. This may include your Social Security card, birth certificate, proof of citizenship, and information about your work history.

4. Attend the Appointment:

- Arrive at the Social Security office at the scheduled time. A representative will guide you through the application process, answering any questions you may have.

5. Provide Necessary Information:

- During the appointment, you'll be asked to provide details about your work history, personal information, and preferences regarding your benefits.

6. Review and Confirm:

- Take the time to review the information provided during the in-person application. Confirm its accuracy before finalizing the submission.

7. Receive Confirmation:

- Upon successful completion, you'll receive a confirmation of your application. This document is important for future reference and tracking the status of your benefits.

Applying in person ensures that your questions are addressed, and you receive personalized assistance throughout the application process. As your advisor, I recognize the value of this face-to-face interaction and encourage you to choose the method that best aligns with your preferences.

5.3 Required Documentation: Building the Foundation for Approval

Ensuring a smooth application process involves having the necessary documentation on hand. Let's explore the essential documents required to build a robust foundation for your Social Security benefits application.

1. Proof of Identity:

- Required Documents: Social Security card, driver's license, or passport.
- Purpose: To verify your identity and ensure the accurate processing of your benefits.

2. Proof of Age:

- Required Documents: Birth certificate, adoption papers, or religious record showing your date of birth.
- Purpose: Establishing your age, a crucial factor in determining benefit eligibility.

3. Proof of Citizenship or Alien Status:

- Required Documents: U.S. birth certificate, naturalization certificate, or immigration documents.

- Purpose: Confirming your citizenship or legal residency status.

4. Proof of Marriage or Divorce:

- Required Documents: Marriage certificate, divorce decree, or spouse's death certificate.
- Purpose: Establishing eligibility for spousal or survivor benefits.

5. Proof of Work History:

- Required Documents: W-2 forms, tax returns, or pay stubs.
- Purpose: Demonstrating your work history and earnings, which directly influence benefit calculations.

6. Bank Information:

- Required Documents: Voided check or bank account information.
- Purpose: Facilitating direct deposit of your benefits into your bank account.

7. Medical Records (for Disability Benefits):

- Required Documents: Relevant medical records, doctor's reports, and supporting documentation.

- Purpose: Substantiating the presence and severity of your disabling condition.

Having these documents in order streamlines the application process and ensures that your eligibility is accurately assessed. As your advisor, I emphasize the importance of thorough preparation, setting the stage for a successful application for Social Security benefits.

6. Social Security and Work: Navigating the Intersection

The intersection of Social Security and work creates a dynamic landscape where individuals can continue employment while receiving benefits. Let's explore how working while receiving benefits can be a strategic choice, providing financial flexibility and empowerment.

6.1 Working While Receiving Benefits: Balancing Act

The idea of working while receiving Social Security benefits may seem like a delicate balancing act, but it's a viable option that offers individuals financial flexibility and the opportunity to stay engaged in the workforce.

Understanding the Basics:

- Earnings Limit: If you are below Full Retirement Age (FRA), there is an annual earnings limit. In 2022, you can earn up to $19,560 without it affecting your Social Security benefits.

Implications for Those Below Full Retirement Age:

- **Benefit Reduction:** If you earn more than the annual limit, Social Security benefits are reduced by $1 for every $2 earned above the limit.

- **Adjustments at FRA:** Once you reach FRA, any reduction in benefits due to earnings is recalculated, and you receive higher monthly benefits.

For Those at or Above Full Retirement Age:

- **No Earnings Limit:** Once you reach Full Retirement Age, you can work and earn as much as you like without it affecting your Social Security benefits.

The Impact of Delayed Retirement Credits:

- **Additional Benefits:** If you choose to continue working beyond FRA, you can earn delayed retirement credits, increasing your monthly Social Security benefits.

Working while receiving benefits is not a hurdle; it's an opportunity for financial empowerment. It allows you to stay active in the workforce, pursue passions, and optimize your overall financial strategy.

Strategic Considerations:

1. Financial Goals:

- Ask yourself: What are your financial goals? Working while receiving benefits can be a strategic move if it aligns with your overall financial plan.

2. Full Retirement Age:

- Consider waiting until Full Retirement Age to avoid benefit reductions. This allows you to earn without impacting your Social Security benefits.

3. Lifestyle and Health:

- Assess your lifestyle and health. Some individuals find fulfillment in part-time or flexible work arrangements during retirement, enhancing both financial and personal well-being.

4. Consultation with Advisor:

- Engage with a Social Security advisor to understand the specific implications for your situation. Tailoring your approach based on professional advice ensures a well-informed decision.

6.2 Earnings Limits and Impact on Benefits: Navigating the Threshold

Understanding the earnings limits and their impact on Social Security benefits is essential for individuals contemplating work while receiving benefits. Let's explore the intricacies of these limits and how they influence your financial landscape.

The earnings limits act as a threshold, determining the delicate balance between work and Social Security benefits. Navigating this terrain requires a clear understanding of the limits and their implications.

For Individuals Below Full Retirement Age (FRA):
- Earnings Limit in 2022: You can earn up to $19,560 annually without it affecting your Social Security benefits.
- Impact of Exceeding Limit: If you earn more than the limit, Social Security benefits are reduced by $1 for every $2 earned above the threshold.

Example:
- If your annual earnings exceed $19,560, Social Security benefits are reduced by $1 for every $2 earned above this amount.

For the Year You Reach Full Retirement Age:

- **Higher Earnings Limit:** In the year you reach FRA, a higher earnings limit applies until the month you reach FRA. In 2022, the limit is $51,960, and the reduction is $1 for every $3 earned above the limit.

After Full Retirement Age:

- No Earnings Limit: Once you reach Full Retirement Age, there is no limit on earnings, and you can work and earn without any reduction in Social Security benefits.

Understanding these thresholds empowers you to make informed decisions about your work and retirement timeline. It's not just about numbers; it's about optimizing your financial strategy for a fulfilling retirement.

6.3 Returning to Work After Retirement: A Second Act

Retirement doesn't necessarily mean bidding farewell to the workforce forever. Many individuals find fulfillment in returning to work after retirement, embarking on a second act that goes hand in hand with continued Social Security benefits.

Key Considerations:

1. No Earnings Limit after FRA: Once you reach Full Retirement Age, you can return to work without any impact on your Social Security benefits. You can earn as much as you want, and your benefits remain unaffected.

2. Potential Increase in Benefits: Returning to work after retirement can contribute to your work history, potentially leading to an increase in your Social Security benefits due to additional earnings.

3. Flexibility and Fulfillment: Returning to work is not just a financial decision; it's an opportunity for personal fulfillment and staying engaged. It allows you to choose work that aligns with your passions and interests.

4. Impact on Taxes: Be mindful of the tax implications of additional income. Consult with a tax advisor to understand how returning to work may affect your overall tax situation.

Returning to work after retirement is a testament to the evolving nature of today's workforce. It's not about age; it's about embracing opportunities for growth, contribution, and financial well-being. As your advisor, I encourage you to explore this second act with enthusiasm, ensuring that your retirement journey aligns with your aspirations.

7. Medicare and Social Security: A Comprehensive Guide

The intertwining of Medicare and Social Security creates a comprehensive safety net for individuals as they navigate the complexities of healthcare and financial security. Let's embark on a journey into the realm of Medicare, starting with an introduction and exploring the eligibility criteria.

7.1 Introduction to Medicare: Bridging the Healthcare Gap

As we delve into the world of Medicare, envision it as a bridge connecting you to essential healthcare services. Medicare, a federal health insurance program, plays a vital role in providing coverage for various medical needs.

Key Components of Medicare:

1. Part A (Hospital Insurance): Covers inpatient hospital stays, skilled nursing facility care, hospice care, and some home health care.

2. Part B (Medical Insurance): Covers outpatient care, doctor's services, preventive services, and some home health care.

3. Part C (Medicare Advantage): An alternative to Original Medicare, offered by private companies and often includes Part A, Part B, and additional benefits like vision and dental.

4. Part D (Prescription Drug Coverage): Offers prescription drug coverage and is provided by private insurance companies.

Enrollment Periods:

- **Initial Enrollment Period (IEP):** Typically starts three months before your 65th birthday and lasts for seven months (three months before, the month of, and three months after your birthday).

- **General Enrollment Period (GEP):** If you miss your IEP, GEP runs from January 1 to March 31 each year, with coverage starting July 1.

Understanding the basics of Medicare sets the stage for exploring its intersection with Social Security benefits.

7.2 Medicare Eligibility: The Path to Healthcare Coverage

Eligibility for Medicare is a milestone in your healthcare journey, ensuring that you have access to essential medical services as you navigate different stages of life.

Age-Related Eligibility:

- **Age 65 or Older:** Most individuals become eligible for Medicare at age 65. This eligibility is not tied to your eligibility for Social Security benefits.

Eligibility for Those Under 65:

- **Disability:** Individuals under 65 may qualify if they have received Social Security Disability Insurance (SSDI) benefits for at least 24 months.

Automatic Enrollment vs. Manual Enrollment:

- **Automatic Enrollment:** If you're already receiving Social Security benefits, you are automatically enrolled in Medicare Parts A and B.
- **Manual Enrollment:** If you're not receiving Social Security benefits, you need to actively enroll in Medicare.

Medicare Advantage and Part D Enrollment:

- **Separate Enrollment:** Enrollment in Medicare Advantage (Part C) and Part D prescription drug plans is a separate process, and you need to actively choose and enroll in these plans.

Understanding your eligibility for Medicare and navigating the enrollment process ensures that you access the healthcare coverage essential for a healthy and secure future. As your advisor, I'm here to guide you through this intersection of healthcare and financial well-being, ensuring that you make informed decisions for your holistic welfare.

7.3 Medicare Enrollment Options: Navigating Your Healthcare Path

Medicare offers multiple enrollment options to accommodate the diverse needs of individuals. Understanding these options empowers you to choose the path that aligns with your circumstances and ensures timely access to vital healthcare coverage.

1. Automatic Enrollment:
- **For Social Security Recipients:** If you're already receiving Social Security benefits when you turn 65, you are automatically enrolled in Medicare Parts A and B. This

automatic enrollment typically occurs three months before your 65th birthday.

2. Manual Enrollment:

- **Not Receiving Social Security Benefits:** If you haven't started receiving Social Security benefits by age 65, you need to actively enroll in Medicare. This can be done online through the official Medicare website or by visiting a local Social Security office.

3. Initial Enrollment Period (IEP):

- **Timing:** Your IEP begins three months before your 65th birthday, includes the month of your birthday, and extends for three months after.
- **For Those Under 65:** If you qualify for Medicare due to a disability, your IEP is based on the 25th month of receiving Social Security Disability Insurance (SSDI) benefits.

4. General Enrollment Period (GEP):

- **Timing:** Runs from January 1 to March 31 each year, with coverage starting on July 1.
- **For Late Enrollees:** If you miss your IEP, you can enroll during the GEP. Keep in mind that late enrollment may result in permanent premium increases.

5. Special Enrollment Periods (SEPs):
- **Qualifying Events:** Certain life events, such as retirement or loss of employer-sponsored coverage, may trigger a Special Enrollment Period, allowing you to enroll in or make changes to your Medicare coverage outside of the standard enrollment periods.

Understanding these enrollment options ensures that you navigate the process seamlessly, securing timely access to the healthcare coverage you need.

7.4 Social Security and Medicare Coordination: A Synchronized Approach

The coordination of Social Security and Medicare is a synchronized dance, ensuring that individuals seamlessly transition into comprehensive healthcare coverage as they reach the age of eligibility. Let's explore the harmonious interplay between these two pillars of financial and healthcare well-being.

1. Automatic Enrollment in Medicare:
- **For Social Security Recipients:** If you're already receiving Social Security benefits when you turn 65, you are

automatically enrolled in Medicare Parts A and B. This automatic enrollment typically occurs three months before your 65th birthday.

2. Coordinated Start Dates:

- **Alignment of Benefits:** The coordination ensures that your Medicare benefits align with the start of your Social Security benefits, creating a seamless transition into comprehensive coverage.

3. Premium Deductions from Social Security Benefits:

- Automatic Premium Deduction: The standard premium for Medicare Part B is typically deducted directly from your Social Security benefits. This automatic deduction simplifies the payment process.

4. Active Enrollment for Non-Social Security Recipients:

- **Manual Enrollment:** If you're not receiving Social Security benefits, you need to actively enroll in Medicare. This can be done online through the official Medicare website or by visiting a local Social Security office.

5. Communication and Guidance:

- Informational Materials: Social Security provides informational materials to individuals approaching the age of Medicare eligibility, offering guidance on the enrollment process and coordination of benefits.

Navigating the coordination of Social Security and Medicare is not just a procedural step; it's a strategic approach to ensuring comprehensive coverage that addresses both financial and healthcare needs. As your advisor, I'm here to guide you through this coordinated journey, ensuring that you transition seamlessly into the world of Medicare, supported by the foundation of Social Security benefits.

8. Common Questions and Myths: Unveiling Clarity

In the realm of Social Security and Medicare, common questions and myths often weave through the narrative. Let's unveil clarity by addressing frequently asked questions, debunking myths, and providing insights to empower your understanding.

8.1 Frequently Asked Questions: Navigating the Landscape

1. Can I work while receiving Social Security benefits?

- Yes, you can work while receiving Social Security benefits, but if you're below Full Retirement Age (FRA), there is an earnings limit. Earnings above the limit may result in a reduction of benefits.

2. When should I apply for Social Security benefits?

- The optimal time to apply for benefits depends on various factors, including your financial situation and health. You can apply as early as age 62, but delaying until Full

Retirement Age (FRA) or even later can result in higher monthly benefits.

3. How are Social Security benefits taxed?

- Depending on your overall income, a portion of your Social Security benefits may be subject to federal income tax. It's advisable to consult with a tax advisor to understand your specific tax implications.

4. Can I receive both Social Security and disability benefits?

- If you qualify for Social Security Disability Insurance (SSDI), you can receive disability benefits until you reach Full Retirement Age, at which point your benefits transition to retirement benefits.

5. How does Medicare work with employer-sponsored insurance?

- If you have employer-sponsored insurance when you become eligible for Medicare, you may choose to enroll in Medicare and coordinate coverage. Understanding the coordination ensures comprehensive healthcare coverage.

6. What is the difference between Original Medicare and Medicare Advantage?

- Original Medicare (Part A and Part B) is a fee-for-service health plan, while Medicare Advantage (Part C) is offered by private companies and combines Part A, Part B, and often Part D benefits. Understanding these options helps you choose the coverage that best suits your needs.

7. Can I apply for Medicare online?

- Yes, you can apply for Medicare online through the official Medicare website. The online application process provides a convenient and efficient way to initiate your enrollment.

8. How do delayed retirement credits work?

- Delayed retirement credits are earned by delaying the start of your Social Security benefits beyond Full Retirement Age (FRA). For each year you delay, you receive an 8% increase in your benefits, up to age 70.

9. Is my Social Security benefit affected if I continue to work after claiming benefits?

- If you claim Social Security benefits before Full Retirement Age and continue to work, your benefits may be subject to an earnings limit, resulting in a reduction for earnings above the limit. After reaching Full Retirement Age, there is no earnings limit.

10. Can I change my Medicare coverage after enrollment?

- Yes, you can make changes to your Medicare coverage during certain enrollment periods. It's essential to be aware of these periods and consider any changes based on your evolving healthcare needs.

Frequently asked questions serve as signposts on your journey, providing clarity and guidance. As your advisor, I encourage you to explore these questions and seek personalized advice to make informed decisions that align with your unique circumstances.

8.2 Common Misconceptions: Dispelling Myths for Informed Decisions

Navigating the landscape of Social Security and Medicare often involves confronting common misconceptions. Let's dispel these myths to ensure that you approach these crucial aspects of your financial and healthcare journey with accurate information.

1. Myth: Social Security benefits are only available at age 65.

- **Reality:** While Full Retirement Age (FRA) for Social Security benefits varies based on your birth year, benefits can be claimed as early as age 62 or delayed until age 70. Understanding the range of claiming options is crucial for informed decisions.

2. Myth: Once I start receiving Social Security benefits, the amount remains fixed.

- **Reality:** Social Security benefits can be affected by factors such as working while receiving benefits, claiming early or delaying, and changes in the cost of living. It's essential to recognize the dynamic nature of Social Security.

3. Myth: I can't work while receiving Social Security benefits.

- **Reality**: You can work while receiving Social Security benefits, but if you're below Full Retirement Age (FRA), there is an earnings limit. Earnings above the limit may result in a reduction of benefits. After reaching FRA, there is no earnings limit.

4. Myth: I'm automatically enrolled in Medicare when I start receiving Social Security benefits.

- **Reality:** If you're already receiving Social Security benefits when you turn 65, you are automatically enrolled in Medicare Parts A and B. If not, you need to actively enroll in Medicare. Automatic enrollment depends on receiving Social Security benefits.

5. Myth: Medicare covers all healthcare costs, so I don't need additional coverage.

- **Reality:** While Medicare provides essential coverage, it doesn't cover all healthcare costs. Many individuals choose supplemental coverage (Medigap) or opt for Medicare Advantage (Part C) to enhance their benefits. Understanding the gaps in coverage is crucial.

6. Myth: I can't change my Medicare coverage once enrolled.

- **Reality:** You can make changes to your Medicare coverage during certain enrollment periods. Open Enrollment, the Annual Election Period, and Special Enrollment Periods provide opportunities to adjust your coverage based on changing healthcare needs.

7. Myth: Social Security benefits are always tax-free.

- **Reality:** Depending on your overall income, a portion of your Social Security benefits may be subject to federal income tax. It's advisable to consult with a tax advisor to understand your specific tax implications.

8. Myth: I must retire from work to receive Social Security benefits.

- **Reality:** You can receive Social Security benefits while working. However, if you claim benefits before Full Retirement Age (FRA) and continue working, your benefits may be subject to an earnings limit. After reaching FRA, there is no earnings limit.

9. Myth: Delaying Social Security benefits is always the best strategy.

- Reality: The decision to delay benefits depends on various factors, including your health, financial situation, and life expectancy. While delaying can result in higher monthly benefits, it's essential to weigh the trade-offs based on your individual circumstances.

10. Myth: Medicare Advantage and Original Medicare provide identical coverage.

- **Reality:** Medicare Advantage (Part C) plans, offered by private companies, may offer additional benefits and have different cost structures compared to Original Medicare

(Part A and Part B). Understanding the distinctions helps you choose the coverage that aligns with your needs.

Dispelling these common misconceptions is a crucial step in building a foundation of accurate knowledge. As your advisor, I encourage you to approach Social Security and Medicare with clarity, allowing you to make informed decisions that enhance your financial and healthcare well-being.

9. Future Outlook and Changes: Navigating the Path Ahead

As we gaze into the future, understanding the dynamics of the Social Security Trust Fund becomes crucial. Let's delve into the current status of the Trust Fund, potential challenges on the horizon, and considerations for navigating the path ahead.

9.1 Social Security Trust Fund: Safeguarding the Future

The Social Security Trust Fund stands as a financial backbone, ensuring the stability and continuity of benefits for millions of Americans. Let's explore its current status and the factors influencing its future.

Key Aspects of the Social Security Trust Fund:

1. Trust Fund Components:
- OASI and DI Trust Funds: The Social Security Trust Fund consists of two parts – the Old-Age and Survivors Insurance (OASI) Trust Fund and the Disability Insurance (DI) Trust Fund. These funds collectively support Social Security benefits.

2. Funding Mechanism:

- Pay-As-You-Go System: Social Security operates on a pay-as-you-go system, where current workers' payroll taxes fund the benefits of current retirees. Any surplus funds are invested in special-issue Treasury bonds held by the Trust Fund.

3. Trust Fund Reserves:

- Current Status: As of the latest reports, the Trust Fund holds substantial reserves. However, projections indicate that these reserves may face depletion in the coming decades.

4. Depletion Projections:

- 2022 Trustees Report: The 2022 Trustees Report projects that the combined OASI and DI Trust Funds will be depleted by 2033. After depletion, payroll taxes alone would cover about 76% of scheduled benefits.

5. Factors Influencing Depletion:

- Demographic Changes: An aging population and a lower birth rate contribute to an increasing number of retirees relative to the number of workers.

- Longer Life Expectancy: The longer life expectancy of retirees places a strain on the sustainability of the pay-as-you-go system.

6. Policy Considerations:

- Potential Changes: Policymakers may consider various measures to address the Trust Fund's sustainability, such as adjusting the retirement age, changing benefit calculations, or modifying payroll tax rates.

7. Public Awareness and Advocacy:

- Informed Decision-Making: Understanding the current state of the Trust Fund empowers individuals to make informed decisions about their retirement plans. Public awareness and advocacy play a vital role in shaping future policies and ensuring the sustainability of Social Security.

While the Social Security Trust Fund faces challenges, it remains a cornerstone of financial security for retirees. Staying informed about potential changes and engaging in discussions about the future of Social Security contribute to a collective effort in safeguarding this essential social program.

9.2 Potential Reforms: Charting the Course for Sustainability

As the Social Security landscape evolves, potential reforms are explored to address the challenges and ensure the program's long-term sustainability. Let's navigate through some considerations and reforms that policymakers may contemplate to secure the future of Social Security.

1. Gradual Increase in Full Retirement Age:

- Consideration: Gradually raising the Full Retirement Age (FRA) is a reform option to reflect increases in life expectancy. This could adjust the age at which individuals can receive full Social Security benefits.

2. Adjustments to Cost-of-Living Adjustments (COLA):

- Consideration: Refining the formula for Cost-of-Living Adjustments (COLA) may be explored to ensure that benefit increases align with actual changes in the cost of living.

3. Changes to Benefit Calculations:

- Consideration: Adjustments to benefit calculations, such as modifying the formula used to determine the Primary

Insurance Amount (PIA), could be considered to address financial sustainability.

4. Phased Payroll Tax Rate Increases:

- Consideration: Gradual increases in payroll tax rates may be explored to enhance revenue for the Trust Fund. This approach could involve incremental adjustments over time.

5. Means Testing:

- Consideration: Introducing means testing, where benefits are adjusted based on an individual's income or assets, is another potential reform to ensure the program's focus on those with greater financial need.

6. Social Security Coverage Expansion:

- Consideration: Expanding Social Security coverage to include more workers who are currently not covered by the program could increase revenue and strengthen the overall financial health of the system.

7. Comprehensive Legislative Overhaul:

- Consideration: Policymakers may explore a comprehensive legislative overhaul to address multiple aspects of Social Security, combining various reforms for a holistic approach.

8. Public-Private Partnerships:

- Consideration: Exploring public-private partnerships to supplement Social Security benefits may provide additional financial resources and options for retirees.

While these potential reforms are considerations on the horizon, it's essential to recognize that any changes to Social Security would involve careful deliberation and consideration of their impact on individuals and the broader retirement landscape.

9.3 Staying Informed: Your Role in Shaping the Future

1. Stay Engaged with Updates:

- Informed Decision-Making: Regularly seek updates on Social Security policies, potential reforms, and changes. Staying informed empowers you to make proactive decisions aligned with the evolving landscape.

2. Participate in Advocacy Efforts:

- Community Engagement: Join advocacy efforts that focus on Social Security sustainability. Active participation in community discussions and campaigns contributes to a collective voice in shaping policy decisions.

3. Seek Professional Guidance:

- Consult with Advisors: Engage with financial advisors and professionals who specialize in retirement planning. Their expertise can help you navigate potential changes and make strategic decisions based on your individual circumstances.

4. Understand Your Benefits:

- Personalized Knowledge: Take the time to understand your specific Social Security benefits, including your Full Retirement Age, potential benefit reductions or increases based on claiming age, and the impact of any future reforms on your benefits.

5. Advocate for Transparent Communication:

- Clarity and Transparency: Advocate for transparent communication from policymakers about potential reforms and changes. Clear information empowers individuals to plan for their retirement with confidence.

Your active engagement and commitment to staying informed play a crucial role in shaping the future of Social Security. As your advisor, I encourage you to embrace your role in this process, contributing to the dialogue and ensuring that Social Security remains a robust and sustainable program for generations to come.

10.1 Social Security Administration (SSA) Website: Your Gateway to Information

The Social Security Administration (SSA) website is a comprehensive resource providing a wealth of information, tools, and services related to Social Security benefits. Navigating this website is key to accessing valuable resources and managing your Social Security journey.

Key Features of the SSA Website:

1. **[Official Website](https://www.ssa.gov/):** The SSA's official website is the primary hub for all Social Security-related information. It offers user-friendly navigation and a wealth of resources.

2. **My Social Security Account:** Creating a [My Social Security account](https://www.ssa.gov/myaccount/) on the website allows you to access personalized information about your Social Security benefits, including earnings history and estimated benefits.

3. **Benefits Planner:** The Benefits Planner section provides tools and calculators to help you estimate your

retirement, disability, and survivor benefits. It also offers guidance on when to claim benefits and how work may affect your benefits.

4. Online Services: The SSA website allows you to apply for benefits, check the status of your application, request a replacement Social Security card, and more through its [online services](https://www.ssa.gov/onlineservices/).

5. Publications and Forms: The website provides access to a wide range of publications, guides, and forms that cover various aspects of Social Security. These resources offer in-depth information about benefit programs and application processes.

10.2 Online Calculators and Tools: Empowering Your Financial Planning

Utilizing online calculators and tools is a proactive step in understanding and planning for your Social Security benefits. These resources help you make informed decisions about when to retire and how different scenarios may impact your benefits.

1.[**Retirement Estimator](https://www.ssa.gov/benefits/retirem ent/estimator.html):** This tool provides personalized benefit estimates based on your actual Social Security earnings record. It allows you to experiment with different retirement scenarios to find a strategy that suits your needs.

2.[**LifeExpectancy Calculator](https://www.ssa.gov/oact/population /longevity.html):** Understanding life expectancy is crucial for retirement planning. The SSA's life expectancy calculator helps you estimate how long you may live based on your current age and gender.

3. [Windfall Elimination Provision (WEP) Calculator](https://www.ssa.gov/planners/retire/anyPia Wepjso4.html): If you receive a pension based on work not covered by Social Security (e.g., from a government job), the WEP Calculator helps estimate how the Windfall Elimination Provision may affect your benefits.

10.3 Social Security Publications and Forms: In-Depth Resources

Accessing publications and forms provided by the SSA is essential for gaining in-depth knowledge about Social Security benefits, rules, and application processes. These resources are valuable references as you navigate the complexities of the system.

1. [Publications](https://www.ssa.gov/pubs/): The SSA offers a comprehensive collection of publications covering various topics, from retirement and disability benefits to Medicare and Supplemental Security Income (SSI). These publications provide detailed insights into program rules and regulations.

2. [Forms](https://www.ssa.gov/forms/): The Forms section of the SSA website allows you to find and download the forms you need for different purposes, such as applying for benefits, requesting a replacement Social Security card, or reporting changes.

10.4 Local Social Security Offices: Personalized Assistance

While online resources are valuable, sometimes you may prefer or need personalized assistance. Local Social Security offices provide in-person services and support.

Visiting your nearest office can be beneficial for specific queries or assistance with complex situations.

1. **[Find Your Local Office](https://secure.ssa.gov/ICON/main.jsp):** Use the SSA's online tool to locate the nearest Social Security office. This tool provides contact information and office hours, helping you plan your visit or get in touch with a representative.

2. **Schedule an Appointment:** While walk-ins are accepted, scheduling an appointment ensures that you receive dedicated time and assistance. Many services can be efficiently handled during a scheduled visit.

3. **[Contact Information](https://www.ssa.gov/agency/contact/):** If you prefer to contact your local office by phone, the SSA website provides a directory of office phone numbers. Calling ahead can help you gather information and ensure a smooth interaction.

Utilizing the SSA website, online tools, publications, and local offices empowers you with the information and support needed to navigate the complexities of Social

Security. Whether you're exploring benefits, estimating retirement income, or seeking assistance, these resources are invaluable in managing your Social Security journey.

11.1 Key Social Security Terminology: Decoding the Language of Benefits

Navigating the realm of Social Security involves understanding key terminology that shapes benefit programs and policies. Let's decode the language of Social Security, ensuring clarity as you explore and plan for your financial future.

1. Full Retirement Age (FRA): The age at which you can receive full Social Security retirement benefits. FRA varies based on your year of birth.

2. Primary Insurance Amount (PIA): The base amount used to calculate your Social Security retirement benefits. It is determined by your average indexed monthly earnings during the highest-earning years.

3. Windfall Elimination Provision (WEP): A provision that may reduce Social Security benefits for individuals who receive a pension based on non-covered work (e.g., government employment) that did not contribute to Social Security.

4. Cost-of-Living Adjustment (COLA): An annual adjustment to Social Security benefits to account for inflation. COLA helps ensure that benefits keep pace with the rising cost of living.

5. Survivor Benefits: Benefits paid to the surviving spouse, children, or dependent parents of a deceased worker who was eligible for Social Security. Survivor benefits provide financial support to eligible family members.

6. Disability Insurance (DI): A component of Social Security that provides benefits to individuals who are unable to work due to a severe and long-term disability.

7. Supplemental Security Income (SSI): A separate program that provides financial assistance to low-income individuals who are aged, blind, or disabled. SSI is not based on work history and is funded by general tax revenues.

8. Medicare: A federal health insurance program for individuals aged 65 and older, as well as certain younger individuals with disabilities. Medicare coverage includes hospital insurance (Part A) and medical insurance (Part B).

9. Social Security Credits: Units used to determine eligibility for Social Security benefits. You earn credits based on your work history and contributions to the Social Security system.

10. Earnings Record: A record of your lifetime earnings on which Social Security benefits calculations are based. It includes information about your annual earnings and the Social Security taxes you've paid.

11. Special Enrollment Period (SEP): A specific timeframe during which individuals can enroll in or make changes to their Medicare coverage outside of the standard enrollment periods, often triggered by qualifying life events.

12. Medicare Advantage (Part C): A private insurance plan that provides Medicare Part A and Part B coverage, often with additional benefits. It may include prescription drug coverage (Part D).

13. Medigap: Medicare Supplement Insurance, often referred to as Medigap, is private insurance that helps cover some of the healthcare costs that Original Medicare doesn't cover, such as copayments, coinsurance, and deductibles.

14. Full Retirement Age (FRA): The age at which you can receive full Social Security retirement benefits. FRA varies based on your year of birth.

15. Primary Insurance Amount (PIA): The base amount used to calculate your Social Security retirement benefits. It is determined by your average indexed monthly earnings during the highest-earning years.

16. Windfall Elimination Provision (WEP): A provision that may reduce Social Security benefits for individuals who receive a pension based on non-covered work (e.g., government employment) that did not contribute to Social Security.

17. Cost-of-Living Adjustment (COLA): An annual adjustment to Social Security benefits to account for inflation. COLA helps ensure that benefits keep pace with the rising cost of living.

18. Survivor Benefits: Benefits paid to the surviving spouse, children, or dependent parents of a deceased worker who was eligible for Social Security. Survivor benefits provide financial support to eligible family members.

19. Disability Insurance (DI): A component of Social Security that provides benefits to individuals who are unable to work due to a severe and long-term disability.

20. Supplemental Security Income (SSI): A separate program that provides financial assistance to low-income individuals who are aged, blind, or disabled. SSI is not based on work history and is funded by general tax revenues.

21. Medicare: A federal health insurance program for individuals aged 65 and older, as well as certain younger individuals with disabilities. Medicare coverage includes hospital insurance (Part A) and medical insurance (Part B).

22. Social Security Credits: Units used to determine eligibility for Social Security benefits. You earn credits based on your work history and contributions to the Social Security system.

23. Earnings Record: A record of your lifetime earnings on which Social Security benefits calculations are based. It includes information about your annual earnings and the Social Security taxes you've paid.

24. Special Enrollment Period (SEP): A specific timeframe during which individuals can enroll in or make changes to their Medicare coverage outside of the standard enrollment periods, often triggered by qualifying life events.

25. Medicare Advantage (Part C): A private insurance plan that provides Medicare Part A and Part B coverage, often with additional benefits. It may include prescription drug coverage (Part D).

26. Medigap: Medicare Supplement Insurance, often referred to as Medigap, is private insurance that helps cover some of the healthcare costs that Original Medicare doesn't cover, such as copayments, coinsurance, and deductibles.

Understanding these key Social Security terms lays the foundation for informed decision-making and effective planning as you navigate the intricacies of the Social Security system.

12.1 Recap of Key Points: Navigating the Social Security Landscape

As we conclude our journey through the intricacies of Social Security, let's recap key points that form the foundation for understanding and optimizing your benefits:

1. Full Retirement Age (FRA): Understand your FRA, the age at which you can receive full Social Security retirement benefits. It varies based on your year of birth.

2. Primary Insurance Amount (PIA): Your PIA is the base amount used to calculate Social Security retirement benefits, determined by your average indexed monthly earnings.

3. Work Credits: Earning Social Security credits through your work history is crucial for eligibility. You need a certain number of credits to qualify for different benefits.

4. Windfall Elimination Provision (WEP): Be aware of WEP if you receive a pension based on non-covered work. It may impact your Social Security benefits.

5. Cost-of-Living Adjustment (COLA): COLA ensures that Social Security benefits keep pace with inflation. Stay informed about annual adjustments.

6. Medicare and Social Security Coordination: Understand the coordinated enrollment process if you're already receiving Social Security benefits when you become eligible for Medicare.

7. Online Tools and Calculators: Utilize online resources, such as the Retirement Estimator, to estimate benefits and plan your retirement strategy.

8. Special Enrollment Periods (SEPs): Be aware of SEPs for Medicare to make changes to your coverage outside standard enrollment periods based on qualifying life events.

9. Local Social Security Offices: Local offices provide in-person assistance. Schedule appointments for personalized support or use online services for efficient transactions.

10. Future Outlook: Stay informed about the Social Security Trust Fund, potential reforms, and changes that may impact the program's sustainability.

11. Advocacy and Participation: Engage in community discussions, advocate for transparent communication, and actively participate in shaping the future of Social Security.

12. My Social Security Account: Create a My Social Security account for personalized access to benefit information, earnings records, and more.

12.2 Planning for Your Social Security Future: Empowering Your Journey

As you embark on your Social Security journey, consider the following steps to empower your planning and decision-making:

1. Personalized Analysis: Analyze your financial situation, health, and life goals to tailor your Social Security strategy. Consider factors like when to claim benefits and how work may impact your overall plan.

2. Professional Guidance: Consult with financial advisors and professionals specializing in retirement planning. Their expertise can help you make informed decisions aligned with your unique circumstances.

3. Continuous Learning: Stay informed about changes in Social Security laws, policies, and potential reforms. Continuous learning ensures that you adapt your strategy to evolving circumstances.

4. Advocacy and Community Engagement: Join advocacy efforts and community discussions about Social Security. Your participation contributes to a collective voice in shaping policy decisions.

5. Regular Benefit Checks: Periodically review your Social Security benefits, earnings records, and other relevant information. Ensure that your records accurately reflect your work history and contributions.

6. Holistic Retirement Planning: Integrate Social Security into your overall retirement plan. Consider how other sources of income, such as pensions, savings, and investments, complement your Social Security benefits.

7. Adaptability: Be adaptable to changes in your life circumstances, health, and financial situation. Your Social Security strategy may need adjustments over time to align with your evolving needs.

8. My Social Security Account Management: Regularly check and manage your My Social Security account. This centralized platform provides easy access to vital information and tools for effective benefit management.

Embarking on your Social Security journey is a proactive step toward securing your financial future. With a foundation of knowledge, personalized planning, and ongoing engagement, you can navigate the complexities of the Social Security landscape with confidence.

APPRECIATION

I extend my sincere appreciation to all those who have embarked on this journey through the intricacies of Social Security. Your curiosity, dedication, and commitment to understanding the complexities of retirement planning have been truly inspiring.

Thank you for entrusting me to guide you through the labyrinth of Social Security terminology, benefits, and planning strategies. Your engagement and enthusiasm in unraveling the nuances of this important aspect of financial well-being have not gone unnoticed.

Special thanks to those who have actively participated in community discussions, advocated for transparency, and contributed to shaping the future of Social Security. Your collective voice and involvement are integral to the ongoing dialogue that influences policy decisions.

Remember, your pursuit of knowledge and financial empowerment is a testament to your proactive approach to securing a fulfilling retirement. May this appreciation extend to the vibrant community that shares a common goal of informed decision-making and a prosperous future.

With gratitude for your engagement and commitment,

BONUS OFFER: FREE AUDIOBOOK!

As a token of gratitude for joining this exploration of Social Security, we're delighted to offer you an exclusive bonus. When you purchase or access the full version of this guide, you'll receive a complimentary audiobook version!

How to Claim Your Free Audiobook:

1. Purchase or Access the Full Version: Ensure you have the full version of the Social Security guide, either in print or digital format.

2. Submit Proof of Purchase: If you've purchased a physical copy, take a photo of your receipt or provide proof of purchase. For digital editions, take a screenshot of your order confirmation.

3. Send Your Details: Email your proof of purchase, along with your preferred email address for audiobook delivery, to lareaderpublishing@gmail.com.

4. Receive Your Audiobook: Once we verify your purchase, you'll receive a link to download your complimentary

audiobook, allowing you to explore the world of Social Security on the go!

This bonus offer is our way of saying thank you for your commitment to financial knowledge and planning. Enjoy the convenience of learning about Social Security wherever life takes you.

Happy listening and continued learning!

Elysian Pinnacle